T0195629

EMPOWERING THOUGHTS

15 Declarations to Stay Focused

TREVIS & PAMELA SNOWDEN

authorHOUSE®

AuthorHouse™
1663 Liberty Drive
Bloomington, IN 47403
www.authorhouse.com
Phone: 1 (800) 839-8640

© 2019 Trevis & Pamela Snowden. All rights reserved.

No part of this book may be reproduced, stored in a retrieval system, or transmitted by any means without the written permission of the author.

Published by AuthorHouse 04/03/2019

ISBN: 978-1-7283-0668-1 (sc)
ISBN: 978-1-7283-0667-4 (e)

Library of Congress Control Number: 2019903788

Print information available on the last page.

Any people depicted in stock imagery provided by Getty Images are models, and such images are being used for illustrative purposes only.
Certain stock imagery © Getty Images.

This book is printed on acid-free paper.

Because of the dynamic nature of the Internet, any web addresses or links contained in this book may have changed since publication and may no longer be valid. The views expressed in this work are solely those of the author and do not necessarily reflect the views of the publisher, and the publisher hereby disclaims any responsibility for them.

Scripture quotations marked NASB are taken from the New American Standard Bible®, Copyright © 1960, 1962, 1963, 1968, 1971, 1972, 1973, 1975, 1977, 1995 by The Lockman Foundation. Used by permission.

We dedicate this devotional to all those who feel that they can not think empowered about where they are in life. The way that you think is of great importance and impacts the way in which you will live your life. Thinking that is not empowered settles for any and everything not understanding that God has so much in store if only your thinking is coursed right. Empowered thinking will set you on a course with God to walk into everything that He has for you. We pray that you will find this book empowering insomuch that embracing it leads you to an empowered way of thinking about your life moving forward!

INTRODUCTION

*We are destroying speculations and every lofty thing
raised up against the knowledge of God, and we are
taking every thought captive to the obedience of Christ.*

-2 Corinthians 10:5

This text of Scripture is telling us that we have to destroy
the things that are opposed to the knowledge of God.
This means that anything that is not in alignment with
what God has said about us needs to be destroyed—it
has no place in our minds. The text says further that we
are to take thoughts captive, forcing those non-Godlike
thoughts to be subject to what Jesus has to say on the
matter. Our thoughts should be subject to Christ, which
means that the thoughts we are having ought to be
thoughts of empowerment because this is what Jesus died
for. He wanted to rid us of the guilty thinking, therefore,
leading us to a place where we think from a place of
confidence and power. For example, in John 6:3-14 which
recounts the miracle feeding of 5,000 plus individuals;
Jesus challenges the thinking of his disciples. All of these
people had gathered together because Jesus has been

teaching and doing extraordinary things among them, and because of His compassion He wanted to feed them. He asked Philipp, one of the twelve, how they could all be feed, why, why. We have to think about this! Why does Jesus ask one of His disciples, essentially, what it would take to feed all these people? Jesus is challenging Phillip to think from a place of empowerment that is not based on the circumstance around you. The disciples wanted to send the people away so that they could go and get their own food in town, but Jesus wanted them to think differently about the situation. This is a running theme (thinking from a place of power) throughout Scripture because God desires that we think the way that He does. Jesus says, "whatever the Father does the Son also does" (John 5:19), which should prompt us to copy the Father the way Jesus did. Furthermore, Joel 3:10 says, "Let the weak say, 'I am strong.'" leaving no room for thinking that is not empowered. So, you see, brothers and sisters that our being made in the likeness of God takes on new meaning when we enter into an empowered way of thinking. This devotional is aimed to assist you in the rebuilding or maintenance of empowered thinking as it will determine how you go about living your life. Enjoy!

DAY 1

I am empowered to do all the things that God
has called me out to do, and I will move
without fear in this. God has placed this
in my heart, and He will see to it that I
succeed. There is no force strong enough
to stop me because God is on my side.
I am empowered by God!

DAY 1

My wife (Pam) and I (Trevis) both were raised in the state of North Carolina, but in different cities (Pam in Edenton and myself in Elizabeth City). This was all that we knew growing up, and it is typical for most people to stay put after they graduate from high school (nothing wrong with this if that's the place where you belong). After graduation in June of 1998, were married the very next day which was June 6, 1998, and lived in Elizabeth City where I grew up. I joined the US Navy in September of that same year, and we remained in North Carolina for over six years. The deployments kept me out often, which is why I think we did not give much thought to moving to another area. It was a topic that came up often at work because I commuted back and forth over an hour each way. The fact that they kept bringing it up was not what bothered me, but that I felt inside that being in Elizabeth City, NC was not where we were supposed to be. But leaving there would go against the norm, right, and not to mention the fear of leaving the ones you've known all your life—most people find it paralyzing to see something like this through.

The issue is really about comfort! See, we grow accustomed to a way of life and get comfortable unwilling to make changes that need to be made. But, it pressed on our heart to the point that we had to look into moving, and when we did an opportunity opened up for us to move to the city of Virginia Beach. You may be thinking, "that is not a big deal," but you would be wrong. We were 24 years old with three children, and one income. We had just enough to move and that was only because my uncle helped us, which made it more affordable to do so. The amazing thing is that the housing that opened up for us normally take months for a family my size, but it happened in a week or two. Not only was the housing a quick turn-around, but considering all that was against us there was total peace about the move. Of course, many people around us had a thousand questions, but God had put it in our hearts to move which for us was the answer to all questions. So many great things have happened to us in this area that affirmed it was the right move for us,

> God had put it in our hearts to move which for us was the answer to all questions.

and that God was with us. We share this piece of our life with you to let you know that you don't have to fear when God places something in your heart to move out on. It does not have to be an actual location move, but simply a move on whatever it is that He is calling you to. We have to be willing to get out of our comfort zones no matter how easy life seems to be going. The reality is that you won't enjoy life to the fullest if you don't take a step of faith outside of your comfort zone.

Abraham faced a similar dilemma when God asked him to leave all his people, and go to a place that he was not familiar with. Genesis 12:1-2 says, "Now the Lord said to Abram,

"Go forth from your country,
And from your relatives
And from your father's house,
To the land which I will show you;
And I will make you a great nation,
And I will bless you,

And make your name great;
And so you shall be a blessing."

He had to leave the place he was most familiar with to go to a place that represented new territory. Many of us can relate to this whether it be a new job, walking away from a job, new business, business closing, location move, educational pursuit, etc. These all represent new places of territory, but when prompted by God through the stirring of our hearts we must exercise trust. Remember, in new territory God is building us up! The beauty in the calling of God (when God places something in you to do) is that He has both a reason and a reward. When you follow the thing that God has placed in your heart (dream, passion, goal, purpose) there is a guarantee that it has meaning and reward. You do not have to be afraid because the one who is stirring your heart up has your back!

DAY 2

I am empowered even in the places where
it seems that I am trapped. Although I can't see
a way out, God is working the situation out
in my favor. I trust God because I am never
in a place where He can't bring me out. I will
witness His miracle working power.
I am empowered by God!

On October 5, 2006 our daughter (Promise) was born, but it was not that simple—never is, and all the ladies said, "Amen!" Promise was a surprise, see, we had our first three children 2 years apart from each other, but here comes Promise 6 years after our third child (Elijah). You see the issue right away I am sure! We thought that we were done after Elijah, but obviously there was a

My husband and I felt trapped… but we determined that this was not the only option—we prayed!

different plan, which we were not aware of. I (Pamela) was having complications that led to Promise being born earlier than she was supposed to, and being preeclampsia was the major reason that the doctors wanted to induce me into labor. Why did they do that? During the labor the umbilical cord got stuck around Promise in such a way that it was causing her heart rate to drop dangerously low. The doctors answer to the problem was to do a c-section on me, which is not what I wanted at all. I have had three deliveries up to this point without any c-sections, and was not about to have this experience—no way!

My husband and I felt trapped, but we determined that this was not the only option—we prayed. We had others we felt were people with a prayer life who cared about us, and in that moment the whole staff involved in my delivery room shifted. Everything changed in an instant, at the snap of a finger, a blink of an eye, and felt like a miracle had truly taken place. Promise was delivered healthy as the other children and without a c-section— praise God! This is one of our life experiences, and an empowering moment because we experienced God in a place where we initially felt trapped and helpless. God is not a respecter of persons, meaning that He could deliver you the way He delivered us from that trapped place.

The Children of Israel faced a situation where they were trapped between the Red Sea and the army of the Egyptians. Exodus 14:9 records, "Then the Egyptians chased after them with all the horses and chariots of Pharaoh, his horseman and his army, and they overtook them camping by the sea..." God had rescued them from Pharaoh who had them enslaved for a long time, but here he is again threatening to put them right back where they were. Does this sound familiar to you? You felt that you had escaped something, but it shows back up again causing you to feel trapped. Why would God lead the children of Israel this way? Why are you where you are right now? God is always a step ahead of your enemies, and only has plans for good in your life despite what you may be going through or what _____ things look like. When you continue to read the 14th chapter of Exodus you find that God performs a miracle by parting the sea, so that the children of Israel could cross over it on dry ground. Who would have thought that this would be the way out? This is why we must trust God even in the places where we feel trapped because God has a plan, and when it unfolds we will be empowered all the more. Our experiences with God take us to greater levels of empowerment until we are living life without fear, with greater confidence, and an awareness of Emmanuel (God with us)!

> **God is always a step ahead of your enemies...despite what you may be going through...**

DAY 3

I am empowered to celebrate not only the times
of obvious victory, but those times where it seems
that I have been defeated. Even when it seems that
defeat will be the end result; I will celebrate. Celebration
will be my response because of all that God has done,
and all that I believe He will do for me.
I am empowered by God!

Over the years I (Trevis) have set goals, and found myself knee deep in working towards those goals that I often forgot to celebrate along the way. One of the most difficult things for me to do is to celebrate, and I say this in the present tense because I

Not celebrating can lead to a downward spiral...

still find this to be a challenge for me. I know that I am not alone in this because there are some of you who are work driven, goal oriented, success focused, etc. These are not bad things, but if you do not pay attention you could miss the opportunities in your work to celebrate. Before long, you will find yourself looking back, and realizing that you never took a moment to celebrate what God was doing in your life. Celebrating is something that my wife (Pamela) got on me about because she saw that I would get tunnel vision regarding my goals, and everything would be all about work from that point on. This was an area of my life that needed improvement, and I am glad that she pointed it out. Not celebrating can lead to a downward spiral because when things go wrong in working towards something; the work driven, goal oriented, success focused, etc. person slides deeper into this non-celebratory state. This is a prime way to set yourself up for depression, and other mental or emotional issues. These things have gripped me more than I would like to admit, which is why I believe that the need for celebration can not be minimized—it is really God ordained!

I can't tell you how often we (my wife and I) thought, "Okay God, when are we going to get the victory here." When our kids were younger we struggled financially like you wouldn't believe. We would take our kids to the park to get our minds off the struggle, and to keep the kids from eating every five minutes—I'm serious. We had fun once we got to the park, but it did not change the reality of what we were dealing with. Over time we learned, my wife better than I, to celebrate while we were in the transition to victory. Today my kids eat like crazy all day long, and we don't have to go to the park in order to distract our minds from financial trouble. When we go to the park it is to enjoy a nice day outside with family, which is the way it should be. The fact that things are different now is a testament to the empowering reality of celebrating. It is not the idea of celebrating itself, but who we celebrate that transitions us from where we are currently to a place of victory. This is why I believe God commanded the children of Israel to celebrate several festivals a year. It was to empower them to focus on what He was doing in their lives, and not the current troubles they were facing. Moses writes in Leviticus 23:4, "In addition to the Sabbath, these are the Lord's appointed festivals, the official days for holy assembly that are to be celebrated at their proper times each year" (New Living Translation). The following were commanded celebrations:

- Passover (Ultimately Salvation and how quick God delivers)
- Pentecost (Ultimately God's presence, joy, thanksgiving)

- Blowing of Trumpets (Reflection on God's forgiveness, and a time of rest)
- Feast of Ingathering (Celebrating the provision of God, individual gratitude).

These are not exhaustive explanations of the feast, but provided in order that you may get a sense of what was being celebrated. The children of Israel were to consider God throughout the year acknowledging His goodness in their lives. We should do the same because it is the heart of God, and it empowers us. You may not feel as though celebrating while in difficulty matters, but we are telling you that it makes a serious difference. The only way for you to know that we are sharing truth is to try it for yourself.

DAY 4

I am empowered because God has blessed me
through Jesus Christ with blessings in heavenly
places. I access those blessings by trusting God,
exercising my faith, and waiting both patiently
and obediently. God's name is on my life, and
with that name Jesus Christ—the blessing.
I am empowered by God!

When I (Trevis) was in the US Navy approaching my 10th year mark a heavy stone rested on my shoulders. The stone was advancing to the next rank, which for me was First Class Petty Office (E-6). I should not have allowed that to happen, but on average people made the E-6 rank

The trusting process was not a walk in the park, but it got easier everyday...

by their 10th year. I was good at what I did, one of the best, but my rate (Operations Specialist) was locked so tight that only a handful of people made rank each time advancement came up. The pressure mounted because this was all that people in my division talked about, and of course humane-nature is to panic, stress, and worry. I had to make a decision to trust God because the reality was that I had done all that I could do to advance on my own: worked hard, studied, and picked the brains of those who made it before me.

The trusting process was not a walk in the park, but it got easier everyday just like anything else we do consistently on a daily basis. Advancement time came around, and I did well, but was shy of advancing by 1 point. I was due an award, which was withheld from me. Get this, it was because I agreed to stay with that command due to their lack of instructors—there was no replacement for me. The award is something they gave to individuals who did well during their tour, and had come to the end of their tour of duty. Of course the person had to be deserving of the award which I was. Needless to say, I was frustrated because I was sure that this was my time, but with my wife's support I stayed focused. The next time the advancement came around I felt like I was a pro at trusting God with this because I had been thorough it before, and what do you know, I made it. I am telling you this because sometimes we feel as if we are not blessed, but nothing could be further from the truth. God wants you to experience His blessings!

Numbers 6:22-27 says, "Then the Lord spoke to Moses, saying, "Speak to Aaron and to his sons, saying, 'Thus you shall bless the sons of Israel. You shall say to them:

> The Lord bless you, and keep you;

> The Lord make His face shine on you, And be gracious to you;

> The Lord lift up His countenance on you, And give you peace.'

> So they shall invoke My name on the sons of Israel, and I then will bless them."

This is what God wanted pronounced over His people, and as you read through the Bible the heart of God on this subject does not change. Set your mind on what God has to say about your life, neither let the difficulties nor the circumstances of life determine how you feel. Feelings are just that, feelings, but we were created by God who is not governed by His emotions. God governs Himself by deciding, and we ought to do the same thing—decide to embrace the truth. You are blessed!

DAY 5

I am empowered to make choices of life, and this
power was given to me by God. I do not have to
make choices of death just because someone
else did. There may have been bad choices
modeled before me, but I choose to make life
choices. I will make life choices for both
myself and those that come after me.
I am empowered by God!

The beautiful thing about being able to choose life is that no one has power over you in that. There are so many things that happen to us over the course of our lives that it's easy to succumb to the idea that we have no choice. I think

A decision away from breaking it... making life choices to do so.

about people who are raised in bad neighborhoods, raised by bad parents, raised in racism, etc. That list can go on for the remainder of this book, but you get my point. These individuals often feel that there is no other choice, but to do what they've seen being done before them. This is where generational issues arise, and we wonder "how can the cycle be broken." The reality is that we are a decision away from breaking it because we are capable of making life choices to do so.

There was a person who grew up mad at the world because their father was absent from their life. Being destructive was their normal everyday life posture because the feeling was that it opened doors for them to get the attention that was desired—the attention they thought they needed. That person did things like making homemade tattoos using needles to carve letters on their arm and causing problems at school. They made trouble for their mom that was not deserved, and all because this person thought that being this way would make them feel better somehow. It took a while which included a lot of beatings (don't act like you never had one) for them to realize that they could choose to do something other than what was being done. They did not have to act the way that they were acting to get the attention sought after, truthfully. What that person did in that destructive state of mind caused pain and was not a blessing to them at all. Living that way was not life at all, and it was all because of the choices that were being made. Realizing that you can choose is life giving and a breath of fresh air! When you are stuck in a death-like mindset it's hard to breath! For that person, changing the way they thought, and choosing life instead not only impacted their life, but that of their children. Could you imagine what their children's lives would be like had

Changing the way they thought, and choosing life instead not only impacted their life, but that of their children

they never decided to make life choices instead of living destructively.

Too often we make choices not thinking of the impact it will make on our children or those who look up to us. Not to mention that fact that we don't consider what those choices will do to us. Deuteronomy 30:19 says, "I call heaven and earth to witness against you today, that I have set before you life and death, the blessing and the curse. So choose life in order that you may live, you and your descendants." The children of Israel had been promised by God that if they would keep His word, life and blessing would be the result they could expect. The word of God is life, and to keep His word is to choose life. What God offers us in His word is life, and if we would take those life-giving words and apply them to our lives, we would truly live. No matter what people say, you have the power to choose life!

DAY 6

I am empowered to do it again despite how difficult it was the first time around. God has equipped me with all the right gifts, abilities, wisdom, power, and grace to do it again. This is why I was able to do it the first time, and it is the reason that I will do it again. I will ignore those feelings of defeat because God has destined me to win.
I am empowered by God!

I (Pamela) have had five kids, and all you ladies know how difficult it is to lose that weight after them babies; say Amen because you know I'm right. It took me a while to get focused on it because life does not stand still so that we can accomplish our goals. I still had to work, at one point, and be both a mother and a wife. As women we tend to focus so hard on our children that we forget to take care of ourselves, or maybe it's just that we are too tired, and have no energy left to do what we need to do for our own lives after we have done everything else. We have to find balance because we have to be able to do all the things that we must to maintain a healthy life. I am not just talking about weight now, but anything that is making your life unhealthy needs to be addressed. I did this for myself and it worked for me! I found balance in my life that enabled me to accomplish my goal of weight loss (52 lbs.).

anything that is making your life unhealthy needs to be addressed.

Don't get me wrong, it was not easy to start. First of all, I was not use to taking time for me the way I should have been doing. Second, I was not use to disciplining myself in this area, but over time it became easier. See, this is what you need to know because we often look at people on TV and think that everything is microwaveable, but that is not the case. When you have been doing something for years, it is more likely that changing will take more time. Don't get me wrong, I do believe in the miracle working power of God that makes the lengthy things shorter in duration. I will tell you that you should look to being committed to making the changes you need to balance your life for better health. We have to stay there once we get there because it's possible to get out of focus as I did. I allowed the stress of life to get me off track, and I am sure that this is not news to you because we all have allowed something to take us out of focus at one point or another. There was so much family drama that I buckled under the pressure and gained all that weight back. You talking about a mad sister, I could not believe that I had allowed myself to go backward from all that success. I felt better, had more energy, and was excited that I actually accomplished what I had set out to do. I am telling you this because I don't want you to feel that you are the only one that has succeeded in something only to be right back where you started. We have the same empowerment from God that we had the first time we experience success in that area. I am on my way back to that weight loss goal, and its God empowering me to that goal. What am I saying? You can do it again!

The children of Israel were used to winning their battles, but against a city called AI they lost and were devastated (Joshua chapter 7). It was something that someone in the family had done, which caused them to lose the battle. In this case it was something that God charged them not to do, which someone did anyway. When this happened God simply removed Himself from the people, which was bad from them sense God was their empowerment (the way in which they experience success). Once they removed the issue they were able to go against AI and defeat them (Joshua chapter 8). What I am trying to say is that when we deal with those things that are in our way of success and health we can walk in the empowerment that God has given. You can do it again!

DAY 7

I am empowered to do big things with small amounts. It is not the amount of money, influence, knowledge, strength, etc., but rather that God is for me. With God backing me the little that I have becomes more than what I need to overcome any obstacle. Nothing can stop me.
I am empowered by God!

The assumption is that you need a whole lot of money, influence, knowledge, strength, etc. to get the things done that you desire, but the reality is that with God you can work from where you are right now. Yes, we did just say that, "where you are right now" because it true! God is not limited because you have little income, are not well known, have little academic acclamation, etc. We don't want people sitting around thinking that they have to wait until all stars align (so to speak) before forward movement can begin, "for we walk by faith, not by sight" (2 Corinthians 5:7). That does not mean that we do things without common sense, but that we trust God as we move forward.

We have talked to so many people who do not move forward in faith because they feel limited by the little that they have, which is only preventing them from getting to the place that they desire to be. As a believer, the place you desire to be is the place where God wants you to be. It is God who placed the desire there such as: the desire to start a church, a ministry, or be a doctor, a lawyer, a teacher, etc. People desire to do the things just mentioned and more, but they feel that they can not move forward because they don't have enough to make those things a reality. These, surely not limited to these, are areas where those desiring such roles can help change the world. *Truth be told, we sometimes don't believe in ourselves enough to take a step forward.* The reality is that God has made us all masterpieces, unique, gifted, etc. We just need to embrace what He has done in us, take heart, and move forward. There was a young man by the name of Gideon who had this problem where he did not think much of himself. He had come from a family that was the least significant within the family tree. You may know what this young man felt like. Perhaps you were raised in a family that others did not think much of; where it did not seem like anyone in your home was doing anything significant. Gideon felt like there were other family households that were doing big things, and had reputation among the other families. Whereas his household was just this poor insignificant household of people not doing much deserving of notice. In fact, he said, "O Lord, how shall I deliver Israel? Behold, my family is the least in Manasseh, and I am the youngest in my father's house" (Judges 6:15). So, not only did he feel that his household was insignificant, but he felt limited because of his age. Gideon thought that because he was young that there was nothing that God could do with him.

It is things like this which cause us to conclude that we can not do big things. We often find things that disqualify us from something that could make a major impact in the world. For Gideon, it was that God wanted to use him to bring about deliverance for his family—not just his household but all of Israel. What is even more interesting about the life of Gideon is that his age was only one thing that he had to get over. Once he accepted what God was trying to do through him he had to come to grips with another reality. That reality had to do with God not needing all those things that we think are needed to do great things. We often think that we need popularity, the highest paying job, the doctorate degree, etc. to get big things done. We have to tell you that these thoughts can be limiting. It is not that you can't desire to be those things that we mentioned, but it is limiting to think that you must be there first before big things can happen. Gideon discovered that God can do big things with small amounts! He discovered this when God wanted him to go up against an army that was oppressing his people. Gideon initially had 32,000 soldiers going into this battle, but God only wanted him to take 300 (Judges 7:1-8). 300 soldiers to go up against over 120,000 soldiers—really (Judges 8:10). As odd as this may seem it is the reality when God is involved. God can do big things through you right where you are, so get your expectation up! Be empowered by this reality, and step out trusting God with the little you have.

> Gideon discovered that God can do big things with small amounts!

DAY 8

I am empowered by the reality that God is a
Restorer, and comforts me in ways that no one
else can. God's love helps me to overcome loss
giving me joy when it seems impossible because
God replaces the pain of loss with His peace. Loss
will not destroy me because I belong to God.
I am empowered by God!

Experiencing loss is like getting the wind knocked out of you, and at the same time there is this bone-breaking pain that comes along with it. So, you feel as if you have a lack of oxygen and, at the same time, as if your body has been crushed all at once. Before moving forward, it must be said that no one can tell you how you feel or how to feel. Loss is different for us all because our relationships are unique to the person we lose. This is just our attempt to describe the feeling of loss when it hit us. We can provide such a description because we have had loss hit our home—our 4-month-old Pamie passed away in 2008. We had 4 children before Pamie, and as a father Pam knew I was very protective in general over my children.

When Pamie came into this world, like my other children, I felt it was my job to protect her. I could also see the bond my wife had with her as all moms do once that baby is placed into their arms. After having four children and seeing them grow the thought of losing them never crossed our minds. After all, everything went smooth for the other children with regard to health, growing, playing, learning, etc. It was the 24th of August in 2008 that we woke up to the loss of our daughter, and the shock is indescribable. How do you cope when you can no longer bond with your child, mother? How do you cope when you can no longer protect your child, father? These are some of the questions that we had to deal with, *but I will tell you that God is a Restorer.* The peace of God is even more indescribable than the shock of waking to the loss of our little girl. Even as we tell you this, you struggle to believe that we came to such a place of peace. It was not counseling of any sort that brought us to this place, but it was God. That is not to knock counseling at all because it has its benefits, but we want to highlight God's peace as it was His peace that helped us overcome the loss of our daughter. The evidence is that we are thriving today, and we can think of her without feeling depressed.

There was a woman by the name of Naomi in the Bible (in the book of Ruth) who had lost her husband and her two sons. She was bitter about this and no one would blame her because loss is tough, and she lost all the men in her household. But, God placed someone (Ruth) in her life that loved her through the pain. It was as if God was demonstrating His love toward her through her daughter-in-law. The book of Ruth is short, read it. What you will find is that Ruth remarries and gives birth to a child whom Naomi was given the privilege of raising as her own. What are we saying in this? That God caused Naomi to overcome her losses, gave her peace, and restored her joy. Ruth 4:15 says, "May he also be to you a restorer of life and a sustainer of your old age; for your daughter-in-law, who loves you and is better to you than seven sons, has given birth to him." God used Ruth and the birth of her son to restore the joy that Naomi had lost. God restored us, He restored Naomi, and He can restore you! God empowers us to overcome loss, and although it may seem impossible, trust Him!

DAY 9

I am empowered to live fearless no matter what is going on around me. I have a covenant with God and because of this covenant I can live free from worry regarding my enemies. My enemies are evidence that I am gifted, talented, loved, good-looking, favored, strong, prosperous, etc.
I am empowered by God!

Here are some synonyms for fearless: bold, brave, courageous, dauntless, doughty, gallant, greathearted, gutsy, heroic (also heroical), intrepid, lionhearted, manful, stalwart, stout, stouthearted, undauntable, undaunted, valiant, and valorous. All of us are often presented with an opportunity to be either fearful or fearless! The good news is that we get to choose which one we will be in any given situation. I (Trevis) remember a moment in my life where I was serving in the U.S. Navy underway on a ship that had supposedly come under attack. An alarm had sounded that everyone was familiar with, and it was made known that it was not a drill. Drills are common out at sea, and no one expects to be under attack after a while because the only thing we become accustom to is drills. What was sounded this time was not a drill, and people were going crazy.

This is what we had prepared for through the drills, but drills don't deal with fear. There were people running, screaming, crying, and vomiting all over the floor because of the fear that had gripped them. I can honestly tell you that in this moment I was fearless (or in this case stouthearted). I was determined not to be afraid, and I am not saying this to make myself out to be better than anyone else. But, in that moment I would not let fear take me over. This is not to say that I have never allowed fear to grip me, but I will say that when I did I discovered that it did not serve me well. When I think of being fearless David comes to mind. He was a small guy and handsome according to the Bible. David was not a part of the army of Israel, but instead watched over his father's flock. If you are familiar with the life of David, you know that he was not esteemed much in his family.

David was an afterthought, and I know many of you reading this can relate. People count you out before you can even be counted in. This sometimes is a contributing factor of our fear—people not believing in us. The reason for this is that we begin to believe what they believe—that we can't do x, y, z. David was determine not to allow what people thought of him dictate whether or not he would be fearless.

In 1 Samuel 16 God instructs Samuel to go and anoint another king in Israel from the house of Jesse. This is the father of David, but when Samuel gets there David is not present because he had not been invited. His family did not think enough of him to consider that he may be the next king that God was talking about. Does this sound familiar? Even Samuel thought that one of the bigger brothers that looked the part would be God's choice, but God corrected him because it was David that God had selected. Side note—God always looks at the heart! David did not allow the fact that he was not invited to the ceremony determine what he would become or how he would be known.

Side note—God looks at the heart!

In 1 Samuel 17 David's brothers go off to fight with a people called the Philistines, and there was a giant (Goliath) in that army talking down to the army of Israel—no one would stand up to fight this man. David's father sends him to check on his brothers, and as soon as he hears the giant taunting the army of Israel he responds. Every Israelite soldier present at that battle was afraid to stand up against that Goliath, but David was fearless. 1 Samuel 17:45 says, "Then David said to the Philistine, "You come to me with a sword, a spear, and a javelin, but I come to you in the name of the Lord of hosts, the God of the armies of Israel, whom you have taunted."" David did not deny how bid Goliath was or his war history, and this is something that we have to learn. We are not saying that you should deny what is in front of you, but to realize that God is for you. *With that you should be able to live fearlessly; not focusing and being controlled by the thing in front of you.* Like David you can live fearlessly because of God, and know that your enemies provide evidence that God has placed so many things within you. Look at your enemies different now, and that will help you in your fearless living!

DAY 10

I am empowered because I am royalty in that I am a child of the King. I am loved, important, destined, valued, cared for, known, etc. (declare more words). No matter where I am right now, I am of royal blood. And by this blood I will live a life knowing that I belong to a kingdom where I have rights. I am empowered by God!

We watched a Creed II trailer, and there was music playing that made a reference to royalty being a part of the DNA. From what we can gather the movie focuses on the son of Apollo Creed (Adonis) as he wrestles with family history relating to his father and Drago (Viktor Drago's father). If you remember, Apollo was killed by Drago in Rocky IV. Although we have not seen the movie, we are betting that Adonis Creed draws from his heritage in training and preparing to fight Viktor Drago. We mentioned all of that to place the focus of royalty on what it should be based on. Royalty has nothing to do with your skin color, last name, credit score, how many degrees you have, the neighborhood you live in, etc. Now, we know that mentioning the credit score one made somebody happy and we could have listed more, but you get what we are saying here. We did not want to take up all of day 10 listing things that have nothing to do with your royal status.

Royalty is based on one thing, your bloodline connection to Jesus Christ! When we discovered this for ourselves it changed everything. The way you see yourself, your past, your future, your children, etc. Knowing from whom you come is empowering especially

> Royalty is based on one thing, your bloodline connection to Jesus Christ!

when you realize that you are a part of the family of God through the blood of Jesus. You are not a subject, but a king or a queen here to exercise that royal right in the earth. Don't look at yourself as helpless, insignificant, poor, worthless, an outcast, weak or any other negative thing that you can think of. The truth is that you are of royal blood, and people of royal bloodlines see themselves loved, favored, special, well known, healthy, wealthy, etc. Think of yourself this way because God takes care of his own.

There was a young man (Mephibosheth) in the Bible who was of royal blood being the grandson of a king (Saul). There was a war that had broken out where he had lost both his father (Jonathan) and grandfather (Saul). He was being nursed at the time of the war, and the person nursing him, for fear of his life, took him away. Now, when this was done Mephibosheth fell in such a way that he became lame by the accident. David had assumed the throne and had remembered a promise that he made to Jonathan, the father of Mephibosheth. He had asked his people if there was any person remaining of the royal family of Saul that he could show them the kindness he promised Jonathan. One of the servants made David aware that the young man Mephibosheth was alive, but lame living in a place called Lo-debar. When David found him, he made a statement that revealed what he thought of himself even though he was of royal blood. He said, "What is your servant, that you should regard a dead dog like me?" (2 Samuel 9:8). Unfortunately, this is how we think sometimes, but the reality is that we are not those negative things. David had to remind Mephibosheth who he was. Not only this, but David restored him to his place and gave him all that belonged to his family. This is what God wants to do with all of us—place us where we belong and restore everything that is ours. Live knowing you are of royal blood!

DAY 11

I am empowered by the miracle working power of God. He is able to work miracles when it comes bondages of sicknesses, lack of provision or finances, mental issues, spiritual issues, etc. The situations that seem to be impossible become possible with God. I expect to see miracles in my life.
I am empowered by God!

My husband (Trevis) and I (Pamela) both have miracles stories of our own, but we also have stories together. Trevis had an ACL surgery to his left knee while he was serving in the U.S. Navy, and was placed on limited duty for a while. After he recovered the Navy attempted to get him orders to full duty, but commands were afraid to take a chance on him. They did not want to take him for fear that he would reinjure himself, which would leave them at a lost with regard to manpower. He finally got orders to a command, but soon after had issues with his knee swelling. He told me that he had woken up one morning and could not bend his knee to walk up the stairs. So, he decided to go to medical to have it looked at. On his way up (several stairs) to medical he remembered how hard it was to get into this command, and considering us (his family) he turned around to head back to his rack (this is what beds are called on ships). He recalled praying to God about it and pouring out is heart about not wanting to be discharged from the service. He laid down to sleep some more before his shift at work, and when he woke up the swelling had gone. He was able to bend his knee, there was no swelling or pain, and it was as if nothing had happened! There is no question that this was a miracle because from what he tells me the swelling was severe and the pain very real. This same miracle working power is available to you!

Both Elijah and Elisha experienced miracle after miracle in the book of 1st and 2nd Kings. The Bible tells of a woman and her son who lived in Zarephath (Sarepta in the New Testament) and were down to their last meal. God had sent Elijah to this family and when he gets there the women is gathering wood to make a fire so that her and her son could make their last meal. When he came across them he said, "Please get me a little water in a jar, that I may drink" but as she was going to do that he said, "Please bring me a piece of bread in your hand" (1 Kings 17:10-11). Now the women had been preparing her last bit of food for her and her son, which she made known to Elijah. Not only this, but she had in her mind that they would die after this because there was no more food in the house for them to eat. The most interesting thing in all this is that God had sent Elijah here to the woman saying, "I have commanded a widow there to provide for you" (1 Kings 17:9).

Of course, God did not mean that the woman would give her last bit of food to Elijah leaving her and her son without. This is evident by what happens after the woman decides to share what she had left with Elijah. The bible records that God spoke through Elijah saying, "The bowl of flour shall not be exhausted, nor shall the jar of oil be empty, until the day that the Lord sends rain on the face of the earth" (1 Kings 17:14). The woman and her son ate from that flour and oil just as God had said through Elijah, and even though it was supposed to be a one-time meal it was sustained by God so that they ate day after day from the same oil and flour. Could you imagine waking up every morning to the cereal and milk that you know you had eaten the day before. Or waking up to eggs, toast, grits or oatmeal every morning knowing that you had eaten that the day before. This was a miracle and there is no question that this miracle strengthened the faith of the women and encouraged the heart of Elijah. Miracles have not stopped and in those places where it may seem that your situation is impossible, God can bring possibility!

DAY 12

I am empowered by prayer because this is where I commune with God. In prayer I share my heart with God, He hears me, and responds to me. Prayer is powerful, full of meaning, and I can expect answers from God. Things come into being when I pray (speaking and listening to God). I am empowered by God!

Prayer has great value, but we have to put it into practice. We must see prayer as something more than a defensive strategy when things are not going well for us. Prayer is just as offensive as it is defensive, but should be primarily offensive because we are to be in prayer with God often. The Bible charges us to "pray without ceasing" (1 Thessalonians 5:17) which means that we are not waiting for something to go wrong to speak with and listen to God. This is what we teach in our home and our children know that God is neither a genie or a slot machine. Prayer with God is the maintaining of a good relationship just as it would take communicating with your children, spouse, boss, professor, etc.

Relationship health is determined by how well the communication is between persons, and this is a fact. One of the number one marriage issues is communication, but this is also true of the other relationships we mentioned before. Prayer is not about being a robot just like it is not about being a robot in any other relationship. It should feel natural to you and you should share honestly and openly with God all that is in your heart. Truth is essential when it comes to communication in relationships! We have had great moments with God in prayer where He has encouraged us, given us wisdom, corrected us, and answered us. There are so many things that we could share with regard to prayer, but there is one thing that happened within the last 2 years that we want to share. We had been praying that we would be able to work together (we don't like

> Relationship health is determined by how well the communication is between persons...

being apart) because the Navy had us away from each other so much. When we were out of the Navy we felt like this was the time from us to gain back that time lost due to deployments. So, we prayed that God would open a door that would allow us to work together. To be honest we were thinking it would be in ministry, and in a way, it is (we have a parachurch type ministry). We do believe that working together in ministry is going to become our only work soon. What happened with regard to us being able to work together started with my employment at Regent University as an Enrollment Counselor. I excelled at the job and was one of the top Counselors in the office. We had been praying and I (Trevis) had been invited to preach at one of our old Pastor's church. During that message, which happened to be about faith, I shared how Pam and I were praying for and believing God that we would be able to work together. It was maybe a month or two after we shared that with the church that an at home job was offered to me. This was one of the most encouraging moments for us because we had been through so much during that time, and when that prayer was answered it increased our faith. ***Don't get caught up in the time, get caught up in God.*** We shared the time simply because it is part of our story. The most important thing to know in prayer is that God is listening and loves you.

In book of 2 Kings there was a king (Hezekiah) who ruled Judah, which was a man that lived for God. This is evident by 2 Kings 18:3 which says, "He did right in the sight of the Lord." It is safe to say that Hezekiah spent time in prayer; that he was a man connected to God. It was not about running to God in times of desperation, but that he had built a relationship with God through prayer. The Bible says further that, "He trusted in the Lord" and "he clung to the Lord; he did not depart from following Him" (2 Kings 18:5-6). All this tells us that Hezekiah had a good relationship with God, and be sure that prayer was a major part of that. Over time Hezekiah had gotten sick and was told by a prophet (Isaiah) of God that his time was approaching to die. When the prophet told Hezekiah that he immediately turned to prayer. This is very telling because our first response in our true response whether it be that we panic, get angry, blame, etc. The fact that Hezekiah prayed tells us that this was his way of life. God answered his prayer and extended his life on earth. What are we saying to you all is that prayer is a vital part of the Christian life, and is without question empowering. It is not just something we do for religious sake, but is something powerful and real! Pray!

DAY 13

I am empowered even in the face of adversity and
when the enemy comes against me God will over-
whelm him. What I begin to rebuild God will help
me finish and cause me to be victorious. There
is nothing that can stop my purpose because what
God has started in me He has purposed to finish.
I am empowered by God!

Adversity is real and every last one of us has experienced it! When it comes we are not supposed to throw our hands in the air and give in to it. We are not facing the adversities we experience in life alone, God is with us (Emmanuel). *Adversity is to battle and the battles that we face do not belong to us, but to God.* It is God who fights for us and our only job is to trust Him as we go through life's adversities. Pam and I spent so much time and energy trying to build a ministry and it seemed like it would never get up and running. There was problem after problem after problem! It started with church life to be honest, and if you are reading this you can relate.

The Church is not perfect, but as the Church we can do a whole lot better because the world sees *Church* worse than the *world* sometimes. After the church issues there was family issues, and after that there was an issue with those we considered friends. It just seemed like it was one thing after the other, and we slowly but surely began to submit those things to God. Slowly, because we often want to handle things ourselves especially when we are frustrated and disappointed. *Understand that adversity gives us an opportunity to exercise our faith in God!* The adversity seemed like it lasted forever, but we are in a place where we have learned to let God fight for us. We established our ministry and are preparing, as we write this, for our first event on November 3, 2018. As you are reading this this event has already happened. This is proof that adversity can not stop you from reaching your purpose, and that what you have started to build God will help you finish all the while overwhelming your enemies.

The Israelites had been exiled from Jerusalem, but

were allowed to return home after being in captivity for a long time. After two years had pass they wanted to rebuild the temple of God because there had been damage due to the war. As soon as they began to build there were adversaries/enemies who opposed the work that they set out to do. First, they asked if they could help having no real interest in supporting them in the building. Do this sound familiar to you at all? Have you ever set out to do something and people acted like they were in favor of it, but actually meant you harm?

The Israelites were smart enough not to agree to let those fake supports assist them in rebuilding. Sense that did not work the enemies cause trouble for the Israelites and discouraged them. They went as far as trying to make the building a national issue sending letters to rulers trying to get the Israelites to stop building. The king of that time replied, "So, now issue a decree to make these men stop work, that this city may not be built…" (Ezra 4:21). This was a setback for the Israelites and we have no doubts that they were frustrated by this. They were working hard, and they were excited to get the house of God back up to standards. The rebuild was held up for two years, but the Bible records that "the eye of their God" (Ezra 5:5) was on them. God was with them and the original documents decreeing that the Israelites could rebuild were found. They were able to start building again and they were given support to finish the building. We are saying to you that no adversity can stop you, and that God has empowered you with purpose to build!

DAY 14

I am empowered both to work and to fight for
what I believe in. All the goals that I have in
my heart or that I have set on paper will come
to pass. I will not give up and I will not give in
until I have accomplished what I have set out to
do. It is possible because I believe it is and
nothing is impossible to those who believe.
I am empowered by God!

We must understand that we are co-laborers with God, which simply means that we have a role to play in our own lives. God is without question with us and helping us through life. There are things that He can do that we can't do, but He has also made it possible for us to participate in our goals, dreams, desires, etc. This is evident by considering the way that God created us; He gave us a soul (mind, will, emotions), a mouth, a brain, arms, legs, etc. Our makeup indicates that we can participate in what God is doing in our lives. Our family have so many individual stories to tell when it comes to putting in work and fighting to reach goals.

Trevis Jr. is working towards a career in entertainment, and has done the following: recorded a single, participated in a movie, and recently acquired a manager with two major auditioning events scheduled. Trying to reach a goal in entertainment can be disheartening because there are so many obstacles and scams, but he is working at it and fighting for what he believes!

We can recall *Tre'shayla* injuring her knee (tore her ACL) playing basketball and being very hurt and disappointed by it. She loves to be active and was determined to not just get back to the courts, but to being active in general. An ACL reconstruction is a challenging surgery to recover from and if you don't fight through it you won't recover properly. We were proud to see her working through the pain to get back to what she loved to do—she recovered nicely!

Elijah had some very challenging years with football, but it is the sport he loves. He had some great years and some years where he did not play as much as he would have liked. None of that kept him from working at his craft and fighting for playing time on the field. He showed so much dedication and hard work throughout the years. We can't tell you his max on the weight bench, his squatting max, or his speed in the 40, but what we can tell you is that looking at him you know that he has put in work to have the build he does. He is currently at Ocean Lakes high school and is starting as running back for the school. So far, they are undefeated, and we are hoping for the State Championship!

Promise wanted to try out for dance last year, so we took her to the studio to register and dropped her off in class. When class was over Promise was so discouraged and it took a while to find out why. She did not want to continue after that session, but we were able to convince her to try another class. The issue was not that she did not like dance, but rather the type of dance for the session she participated in the first time. There was another type that she tried the very next day and loved. She is dancing this year and we shared that because sometimes we run from what we want to do because we think that there is no other way to do it. These may seem like small things to you, but for our children these are some major goals and victories. They are working and fighting for what they believe in, and we trust God that they will accomplish all they set out to do.

Nehemiah and the people of Israel wanted to rebuild a wall around the city, but some people were against them having this wall up. They literally had to fight for this wall and very last person was willing to work together to get it done. The Bible says, "Those who were rebuilding the wall and those who carried burdens took their load with one hand doing the work and the other holding a weapon" (Nehemiah 4:17). They were dedicated to getting that wall up that they worked and at the same time held a weapon to fight off those who would oppose. This is the attitude that we have to have when we are trying to achieve something. Not only did the people of Israel work and fight, but they trusted God through the process. We understand that out own efforts are not enough, which is why we said in the beginning that we are co-laborers with God. Trust God as you work towards your goals and know that it is possible to achieve them!

DAY 15

I am empowered because I am favored by God
and what may not work for someone else will
work for me. Gods favor surrounds me like a
shield not only opening doors but protecting
me as well. By Gods favor I am able to stand
before people in high positions with influence.
I am empowered by God!

Favor is defined as approval, support, or could refer to an act of kindness beyond what is due or usual. When God places His favor on you there is nothing that anyone can do to stop what He has for you. Some people do not like the idea of favor, but that's only until they are the ones being favored. Favor goes a long way, especially because we do not always deserve favor from God. Thankfully we do not have to be perfect to experience God's favor! We do believe that a well lived life in Christ is rewarded, but again we do not always deserve what we get in life, and this is God's favor at work. We honestly believe that we experience the favor of God often in our lives. Often, we are pointed out from among the crowd being pulled from the back to the front—so to speak. We have been kept safe from many dangers both aware and unaware of. Instead of sharing another story here though, we want to focus on the importance of your thinking as it pertains to God's favor.

We live each day knowing that we have favor, which really speaks to the way we think. Not that we have everything all together or are better than anyone else, but that we have learned to expect God's favor every day. Expecting favor requires you to think empowered otherwise you will live within the confines of where you are. For example, someone may grow up in a family that simply does not have the resources to send them to college, audition for a role that others are more qualified for, interview for a job that others have more experience to do, etc. If these individuals think according to their situations then they would remain confined, but empowered thinking allows you to embrace the favor

73

that God declares is on you. Now, this favor can become a recognizable reality in your life that others can see. The favor of God is there, but unexperienced because people do not expect it based on their current situations or the lack that they have always known. *God wants to have you pulled from the crowed to do something extraordinary, so begin to think empowered!*

In the book of Esther, Esther (Hadassah-Hebrew name), was selected as one of the virgins to appear before the king (Xerxes). The king had sent his wife (Vashti) away because of her disrespect for the king. This was something that he had to do in order to maintain the respect of his peers, but he was bothered by it. So, his servants had suggested that virgins be brought in to see which one the king would select. I know what you all are thinking, but these were different times. The culture of this time was much different from the one we know today, so don't stress this aspect of the story. All of this had purpose and an ultimate goal was reached. Because of God's favor Esther was selected by the king as the one who would essentially replace his former wife. This may seem insignificant, but from this new position Esther was able to save her people (the Hebrews) from a plot where all Hebrews would be killed. Out of all the virgins that had been brought before the king it was Esther that was selected. This was not a coincidence, but God giving her favor before the king. Not only was Esther favored, but her uncle Mordecai was as well. He also was a Hebrew, but that did not stop the king from honoring him above those of his own people. The king skipped over notable people within his own palace to honor Mordecai in front of everyone. What are we saying? We are saying that God's favor picks you out of the crowd, and gains you favor among those who should not even be interested in you because there are others that were thought to be before you, but God!

CONCLUSION

*For God hath not given us the spirit of fear; but
of power, and of love, and of a sound mind.*

-2 Timothy 1:7

It is the heart of God that all of us have a sound mind,
which is a part of having empowering thoughts! We hope
that as you have read through this book you have sensed
this truth because it was our aim. At some point we all
have experienced a soundless/powerless mind and can
admit that it was not a great experience. It's always better
to live with a soundness of mind than a soundlessness of
mind! Having said that, let us focus on being sound of
mind as it will lead to empowering thoughts and a better
life. A better life not only for ourselves, but for those
coming up after us. One of the most challenging things
to do is to overcome a wrong way of thinking. This is
especially truth when you have been programed to think
one way for a long period of time. We want the best for
you and so does God, but we have to take up empowered

thinking. If we do not take up an empowered way of thinking, we miss out on what God wants to do in our lives. A sound mind is a mind empowered, embracing all that God says about them and living fearlessly.

ABOUT THE AUTHOR

Trevis and Pamela Snowden are founders of Trevis & Pamela Ministries and have been serving in ministry for over 11 years. They both attended Regent University in ministry programs to obtain both a Bachelor's and Master's degree. They have been married for 21 years now, and have 4 children (Trevis Jr, Tre'shyala, Elijah, Promise). Baby Pamela was their 5th child, but she passed away in August of 2008. They have marriage experience, parenting experience, ministry experience, college experience, etc. and know personally that it takes an empowered way of thinking to get to the places that God wants you in life. In this book, they share from those aforementioned experiences to encourage their readers to think empowered.

Printed in the United States
By Bookmasters

Printed in the United States
By Bookmasters